The Essential Guide

to Hadrian's Wall Path National Trail

2004

Compiled by National Trail Officer
David McGlade

Published 2004 by the Hadrian's Wall Path Trust

ISBN: 0-9547342-0-3

A large print version is available, contact the National Trail Officer, The Countryside Agency, Cross House, Westgate Road, Newcastle upon Tyne, NE1 4XX.

If you have any comments or suggestions for the 2005 guide please write to the National Trail Officer.

Every effort has been made to check that the information in this guide is accurate at the time of going to print. The publishers cannot accept responsibility if opening times or arrangements are different to those advertised.

Printed on Revive Recycled stock. Designed by Differentia Ltd, www.differentia.co.uk.

Many thanks to Mark Richards for the use of the photographs on the front and back covers.

Thanks go to the Countryside Agency for funding this publication.

Contents

Foreword

I am very pleased to write this Foreword to the essential guide. Hadrian's Wall is a wonderful place to be for all sorts of reasons. Central is the archaeological monument which was inscribed as a World Heritage Site in 1987, recognising its universal importance in the history of the human race. The Wall runs through a very varied and inspiring landscape ranging from the tranquillity of the Solway Estuary to the rugged uplands of the central part of the Wall. It is rich in flora and fauna and geological variety. Yet the visitor's experience of even the most magical places can be marred if there is nowhere to get a cold drink on a hot day or it is difficult to find a hearty meal in the evening after a long day's walking the National Trail - and even worse if you cannot find a place to withdraw cash to pay for these! This guide will greatly help walkers and visitors to find such mundane but nevertheless essential services, and so help you to enjoy Hadrian's Wall to the full.

Hadrian's Wall is a very special place, the northernmost part of the frontier of the Roman Empire that stretched across three continents from the Irish Sea to the Atlantic coast in Morocco. Its age and nature also makes it fragile. In places the Trail passes on or near sensitive archaeology and it is essential to keep these remains for future generations to enjoy as much as, if not even more than, you have. By following the advice of the code "Every Footstep Counts" and the "Conservation Tips" you can help preserve this wonderful asset.

Paul Austen
Co-ordinator, Hadrian's Wall World Heritage Site Management Plan.

Introduction

This is the first Essential Guide to the everyday facilities and services needed by walkers following Hadrian's Wall Path National Trail. It has been compiled in response to the many little grumbles and complaints from last year's Trail users who sometimes found themselves without funds, water, food or transport to their accommodation. The guide is a list of where things are, their opening times and position relative to the Trail, and it will try to put you in touch with the businesses and services along the way. It attempts to paint as full a picture as possible but sometimes it points you in the direction of other sources of information; do send away, for example, for the leaflets and guides that we recommend in the publications section and check the National Trail website from time-to-time (www.nationaltrail.co.uk/hadrianswall) for the latest news and information.

When planning your walk, have a look at the top tips offered by last season's walkers. Sit down with your walking companions, together with maps, guides and public transport information, and work out where you intend to be at the beginning and end of each day. Learn where and when the buses connect with the route, likewise note the locations of the water taps and WCs, cafés, pubs and cash-points etc. and plan your itinerary accordingly. With good planning you will avoid the unnecessary gnashing of teeth that many unprepared walkers experienced in 2003! So many of them found themselves faced with another tiring trek at the end of an already long day's walk - many a B&B owner reported having to peel them, exhausted, off the ground at the end of it, and several ended up having to drive walkers to a cash-point machine the next day in order that they could obtain funds to pay for their board and lodging.

If you would like to recommend additional entries for next year's guide please make a note of them as you go along and let us know about them. Have a great walk!

All the lists in the guide work from east to west, that is, from Wallsend to Bowness-on-Solway

Hadrian's Wall is a very sensitive place, a fragile piece of our heritage. Almost everywhere that you walk is archaeologically important. The many excavations have shown this to be the case, so we all have a responsibility to make sure that the surviving remains are preserved for future generations. Hadrian's Wall Path seeks to achieve an appropriate balance between the needs of recreation, conservation, economic development and farming.

When the National Trail received government approval for its creation it was decided that it should be managed as a green sward path. A green sward, or grass path, is important for three reasons. Firstly, by maintaining a green surface and not damaging or breaking into it, any buried archaeological deposits will be protected. Secondly, it provides the most sympathetic setting possible for the Wall and its associated earthworks, and finally, a grass path is the most pleasant of surfaces to walk upon.

This decision, which is supported by English Heritage, means that the management and marketing of Hadrian's Wall Path differs somewhat from that of most recreational routes elsewhere in the UK. A grass path clearly cannot take as much pressure from visitors' feet compared to one that has been engineered, and in the wet winter months it is especially vulnerable to damage. So too is the archaeology. For this reason, the need to protect the very thing that people come from all over the world to visit, the National Trail is promoted only as a spring, summer and autumn destination, but not as a winter one. We hope that you will understand, therefore, why our National Trail passport season runs only from the 1st May to the end of October each year. You can collect your passport stamps only within this period (see page 10).

By walking the Trail in the drier months, you will make a significant contribution to the well-being of the World Heritage Site. The latter actually has its own code of respect, called Every Footstep Counts (see below, also Publications section), it is also on our website (www.nationaltrail.co.uk/hadrianswall). Please do your best to follow the code, by doing so everyone connected with the Wall will appreciate your help.

Other ideas for visiting the Wall in the winter months

We do, of course, still welcome you to the region in the winter. However, the Trail itself is not promoted as it basically needs a rest so that everything can recover in time for the following spring season. There are still several Roman sites that remain open in winter, they are more robust and can better withstand visitor pressure. Likewise, there are many walking routes where you will discover the spirit of Hadrian's Wall country. To offer walkers alternative walking suggestions, therefore, the Countryside Agency and Heritage Lottery Fund have sponsored the production of more than forty promoted circular and linear walks within the Wall's corridor. A leaflet summarising all of these walks is available, see the publications section on page 16.

These corridor walks will soon have their own **winter passport** that will operate from the 1st October 2004 to the 30th April 2005. The idea is the same as for the National Trail passport except that the stamping stations will be in cafés and other businesses located on the circular walks. Collecting a set number of stamps will also qualify a walker for an exclusive winter achiever's badge. We will announce news of the winter passport on the National Trail website (www.nationaltrail.co.uk/hadrianswall).

When you are out on the Trail there are a couple of **very simple things** that you can do that will not only help to **conserve** the historic landscape, but also protect farmers' grazing land and give you a more pleasant surface to walk on. Everyone wins!

Please keep off the wear line

Tip number 1

When you see a worn line in the grass, instead of walking on it, please simply walk alongside it. We actually want you to make full use of the available path and by doing so you will help to conserve the archaeology underfoot. The thing to avoid at all costs is bare earth, once that happens the grass is unlikely to recover. Whilst walking the Trail you will occasionally come across small notices as reminders to keep out of the worn lines in the ground.

Please keep off the ridge

Tip number 2

The Trail's precise alignment was designed so as to avoid sensitive archaeology, the basic rule of thumb was to avoid as many of the lumps and bumps as possible. In the main, the path tries to follow level ground and it has been waymarked as such. Sometimes, however, you might be tempted to seek a better view by walking on an adjacent grassed ridge or a piece of raised ground but, if you do, you will almost certainly be walking on a sensitive archaeological earthwork. So, the second tip is that you should normally walk on level ground and avoid the temptation to walk on anything that resembles a ridge.

Tip number 3

Simply, please resist the temptation to walk on Hadrian's Wall itself. The legal right of way is on the ground alongside the Wall and there is the added risk of injury from tripping on the uneven surface - the casualty department in Hexham hospital will testify to the walkers taken there each summer. Hadrian's Wall is, moreover, a sensitive monument, indeed parts have almost no load bearing capacity at all, and from time-to-time sections do collapse. Please do your bit to help conserve it for future generations by admiring it from alongside. Thank you.

Every Footstep Counts

The World Heritage Site's very own country code

(The code is also on the Trail's website - www.nationaltrail.co.uk/hadrianswall). All of the organisations associated with the care and management of Hadrian's Wall World Heritage Site have signed up to the following code. Please do your bit to help them protect it for future generations.

- The risk of erosion to this historic monument is at its greatest during wet winter conditions, particularly between November and April. Alternative circular walks close to the Wall have been specifically designed and are advisable during these times. They allow walkers to experience the stunning and dramatic scenery of the World Heritage Site whilst preserving the Wall, its earthworks and surrounding environment.

- Start and finish your walk along the Wall at different places, or follow a circular route. Details of some of the huge range of walks are listed in the leaflet Walking Around Hadrian's Wall (which also contains this code - see page 16). Allow extra time to visit the Roman forts and museums and other attractions in Hadrian's Wall country. Information on all walks, attractions, accommodation and events is available from the Hadrian's Wall Information line (telephone 01434 322002).

- Please don't climb or walk on top of Hadrian's Wall.

- Camping is allowed on official sites only.

- Support people living and working in the World Heritage Site by staying nearby, and use local shops, restaurants and pubs. You will be most welcome and will get a real flavour of the area.

- Take any litter away with you and never light fires.

- Close all gates behind you, unless it is clear that the farmer needs the gate to be left open.

- Keep to paths signed from the road with coloured arrows or the National Trail acorn symbol.

- Please keep your dog under close control, in fields with sheep this means on a lead. On National Trust property it is compulsory to keep your dog on a lead.

National Trail passport

Between May and October each year, collect all six stamps in the passport from the stamping stations to qualify for the exclusive Hadrian's Wall Path completion badge and certificate. Purchase the badge (£2.95) from either Segedunum Roman Fort in Wallsend or the King's Arms in Bowness-on-Solway or by mail order from the Hadrian's Wall Information Line. Send completed passports and a cheque for £2.95 (made payable to Tynedale Council) to: Haltwhistle Tourist Information Centre, Railway Station, Station Road, Haltwhistle, NE49 9HN. Tel: 01434 322002. Email: haltwhistletic@btconnect.com

Segedunum Roman Fort - start of Trail. Situated inside main entrance of the museum. Available normal opening hours (see list of historic sites).

TOTAL petrol garage. 150 yards east of Segedunum. Open Mon - Fri 07.00 to 21.00; Sat 07.00 to 20.00; Sun 08.00 to 20.00.

Robin Hood Inn - 1 mile (1.3 km) west of Whittledene Reservoir. Grid ref: NZ 050 684. Situated on right hand side of porch entrance. Available anytime.

Chesters Roman Fort - (Chollerford) Grid ref: NY 911 704. Situated inside main entrance of museum. Available standard English Heritage opening hours. When site is closed an outside stamping box will be displayed on the site building.

Birdoswald Roman Fort - Grid ref: NY 615 663. Situated inside main entrance and shop. Available normal opening hours. When site is closed an outside stamping box will be displayed on the site building.

Sands Sports Centre - Carlisle. Grid ref: NY 402 565. Situated inside centre café - access via glass door from Trail on riverside path. If locked access at front of building. Available during normal opening hours (see page 57).

The Banks Promenade (or the King's Arms) - Bowness-on-Solway. Grid ref: NY 223 628. Situated at the very end of the Trail. Available any time. Available at the Kings Arms during normal opening hours (see page 62).

Organisers of large groups or charity events

If you are organising a walk for a large group or for a charity event the following tips are for your guidance. The advice attempts to strike a balance between our need to manage and conserve the Trail and World Heritage Site, and your desire for an enjoyable walk.

1. The National Trail project cannot, at the moment, offer you a guiding service. If you require an experienced guide please consider one of the walking operators listed in the 2004 Accommodation Guide. (See page 16).

2. It is vital that you familiarise yourself with the Trail long before the actual event. Do be aware of the terrain and think about the abilities of your walkers. In 2003 many groups either underestimated the difficulty of the walk or overestimated their own abilities.

3. Please plan your walk for the drier months of the year, between May and October. Avoiding the wet winter months will help to prevent erosion to both the Trail and monument. (See page 6).

4. Do let the National Trail Officer know that you are planning an event. You will be given as much advice and help as possible.

5. A party of 50 is considered to be a reasonable upper limit for an event walk; during the peak season larger groups may encounter parking congestion at some places used as check points. Remember that your large group may not be the only one on the Trail at any one point in time.

6. Note that there is absolutely nowhere to park in either Port Carlisle or Bowness-on-Solway. Taking a coach into the latter has, in the past, caused chaos there.

7. Be aware of where all the WCs, water taps and other facilities are. Please avoid knocking on private occupiers' doors to ask for water.

8. Read the top-tips section for good general advice!

Top tips - check list

The following tips and suggestions were offered by our first summer season of walkers in 2003. They should stand you in good stead for your walk along the National Trail. (Any further tips for the 2005 edition will be gratefully received!).

1. Book your accommodation beforehand. If you turn up without a booking during the main season you risk being disappointed.

2. Carry a cheque book. Very few small accommodation addresses accept debit and credit cards. Also, plan ahead and note where the many banks, cash point machines, Post Offices and shops that provide a cash-back service are. (See page 38).

3. It is not an easy walk. Some guidebook and magazine articles have described the Trail as "not a challenge walk" but it is much more difficult than many people imagine it to be. The section between Chollerford and Birdoswald, some 23 miles and for the most part a switchback with seemingly endless ups and downs, usually sorts out the fit from the un-fit.

4. Know where you can access public transport and carry the necessary timetables.

5. The quietest time for visitors during the summer is outside of the school holidays. This means avoiding the last week of July, all of August and the first week of September.

6. In the interests of conserving the Path and ancient monument, the best time to walk the Trail is from May to October. This is the time when the ground is normally drier and able to withstand the pressure of thousands of pairs of feet. The Trail passport also operates only during this period. (See page 10).

7. If you are an independent traveller the best time to walk the Trail is when the AD 122 Hadrian's Wall bus operates a daily service, as it connects the route with most of the nearby towns and villages. The daily service will operate in 2004 between 29th May to 26th September; outside of the main bus season you will find it more

12

difficult to plan your itinerary. Send away for the public transport guide. (See page 16).

8. When booking accommodation check to see if a pick-up and drop-off service is provided.

9. Most people begin their holiday on a Saturday or Sunday. By starting on a weekday you might avoid some of the crowds and find it easier to book your accommodation.

10. Carry your mobile phone with you. Use it to phone ahead to order sandwiches from the many cafés or to meet your pre-arranged pick-ups.

11. The occasional Internet facility along the Trail is useful for checking the weather forecast, and for 12 below (check the other lists for Internet cafés and other Internet access).

12. Make sure that you know when the Solway marshes are likely to be subject to tidal flooding. (See page 25).

13. If you use the Tyneside Metro have change ready for the ticket machines, there are no ticket offices at the stations.

14. The route is very exposed to the sun and there is very little shade to be had. Carry a hat and sun screens.

15. If you are a member of either English Heritage or the National Trust, remember to pack your membership cards as there are several sites in the area.

16. Midges can sometimes be a problem! Carry a suitable insect repellent.

17. The 12 miles on Tyneside are on Tarmac paths that can be unforgiving on your feet. You might prefer to wear soft shoes or trainers for this section. In any case carry a blister repair kit.

18. Don't forget to pack your map and/or guidebook!

Frequently asked questions

How long? The Trail is 84 miles, or 135 kilometres, long.

East or west - which is the best way to walk? Eastbound walkers start on the quiet Solway estuary and finish in the bustling city, westbound walkers do it the other way around. It is, of course, a matter of opinion, however, the National Trail Officer's personal preference (having walked it in both directions) is to start in Wallsend and head west. Many walkers agree, an often-heard comment in 2003 was that the landscape "gets better" the further west you go. Certainly, the Solway is a most pleasant place to reflect on one's experiences at the end of a long journey.

We are often asked about the prevailing wind and whether it is better to walk with it on your back instead of in your face. Well, in the peak summer months (June to September) the wind is usually fairly benign so it normally shouldn't make that much difference.

How many days should we take? If you are an experienced walker, used to walking for several days at a time, then six days should be enough for you to walk the Trail. If, however, you are less experienced you should allow much more time or you will find it difficult to visit any of the Roman Wall sites. In 2003 many people overestimated their ability and B&B landladies reported having to virtually peel people off the ground at the end of a long hot day.

Are there enough campsites? At the moment it is difficult to rely upon campsites only, so many walkers use the camping barns and youth hostels for the occasional night. **We do ask you, however, not to wild camp,** it causes problems for both Trail staff and farmers. In the fullness of time more campsites will open for business but this is still early days for the Trail.

Is it easy to follow? The Trail is clearly signed, and waymarked with the standard National Trail acorn symbol and waymark arrows.

On Tyneside, why is it called Hadrian's Way? This is the local name for what was originally a city cycleway. The name simply stuck so the Trail project decided to leave things the way they were. It is, however, still signed with the acorn symbol.

What are the best publications? See page 16.

Latitude and Longitude? A few people in 2003 asked for this information, so for the record:

Segedunum Roman Fort at Wallsend:	Latitude 54°: 59": 3' north
	Longitude 1°: 31": 7' west
Bowness-on-Solway:	Latitude 54°: 57": 2' north
	Longitude 3°: 12": 7' west

Are there any walking operators?

There are several firms that arrange accommodation, guided and self-guided itineraries along the Trail. A full list of operators is to be found in the 2004 Accommodation Guide. (See page 16).

Is there a baggage handling service?

Some of the walking operators will arrange to move your bags for you each day. At the time of writing, however, there is only one firm providing a service for the independent traveller. The Walkers' Baggage Transfer Company currently charges £5 per bag moved and can be contacted at 0870 990 5549. www.walkersbags.co.uk

Is there much road walking?

No, but do take care at the road crossings. There are several crossings along the section between Heddon-on-the-Wall and Chollerford.

Recommended publications

The Trail itself

Before you start planning your visit to Hadrian's Wall Path you will need a map or guidebook. At the moment we recommend two publications, the official Aurum Press guidebook and the Harvey strip map. Both will escort you along the Trail but which one to use is a matter of choice, some walkers carry both. The guidebook is a detailed description of the route with Ordnance Survey strip maps at 1:25,000 scale while the Harvey map is at 1:40,000 scale with a few sections enlarged for additional clarity. It also includes some interpretive information.

You might prefer a set of four Ordnance Survey maps which have the added advantage of showing the Wall and Trail in their wider context.

The official guidebook, *Hadrian's Wall Path* by Tony Burton (2003), is published by the Aurum Press. £12.99. ISBN 1 85410 893 X.

The Harvey strip map, *Hadrian's Wall* (2003) is published by Harvey. £8.95. ISBN 1 85137 405 1.

Ordnance Survey maps. Four Explorer map sheets at 1:25,000 scale are necessary for the Trail, at £6.99 each, as follows:

Explorer sheets 314 (Newcastle); 315 (Solway); 316 (Carlisle); plus the Explorer (OL) 43 (Hadrian's Wall).

In addition to the above, the **forthcoming guidebook** is also due to be published in spring 2004: *Hadrian's Wall* by Mark Richards, published by the Cicerone Press will cost £12.00. ISBN 1 85284 3926.

Other 'must get' information

Send away to the Hadrian's Wall Information Line (01434 322002; e-mail haltwhistletic@btconnect.com) for the following free guides:

• 2004 Accommodation Guide;

• Walking around Hadrian's Wall - lists more than 40 promoted walks within Hadrian's Wall country. It also contains **Every Footstep Counts**, the World Heritage Site's code of respect.

- 2004 Summer Guide, which contains the essential public transport timetables (See page 20).

The Information Line is also a Tourist Information Centre and stocks all the available information about the Wall, Trail and World Heritage Site.

Background reading

If you would like to read around the history and archaeology of Hadrian's Wall we recommend the following:

Hadrian's Wall by David Breeze and Brian Dobson (2000); Penguin. £9.99. ISBN 0 14027 1821.

Hadrian's Wall by David Breeze (2003); English Heritage. £3.99. ISBN 1 85074 834 9. This is the second edition of this popular souvenir guide, updated and lavishly illustrated.

Recommended bookshops

For a reliable service we recommend that you consider using one of the following:

1. For mail order telephone sales (credit and debit cards) contact the Hadrian's Wall Information Line on 01434 322002. Address: Haltwhistle TIC, Railway Station, Station Road, Haltwhistle, Northumberland, NE49 9HN. E-mail: haltwhistletic@btconnect.com

2. For Internet sales contact the Offa's Dyke Centre Internet Bookshop. For many years the Offa's Dyke Centre has served the needs of walkers using the Offa's Dyke Path National Trail, it now sells guidebooks for all of England and Wales' National Trails via a secure Internet facility (www.offasdyke.demon.co.uk).
Address: The Offa's Dyke Centre, West Street, Knighton, Powys, LD7 1EN Telephone: 01547 528753. E-mail: offasdyke.demon.co.uk

Websites

Key websites of interest to walkers:
www.nationaltrail.co.uk/hadrianswall
www.hadrians-wall.org

Distance Calculator (miles)

	Wallsend	Tyne bridge	Heddon	A68 Errington Arms	Chollerford	Housesteads	Steel Rigg	Greenhead	Gilsland	Walton	Newtown	Crosby	Carlisle	Burgh-by-Sands
Wallsend														
Tyne bridge	5													
Heddon	15	10												
A68 Errington Arms	25	20	10											
Chollerford	30	25	15	5										
Housesteads	39	34	24	15	10									
Steel Rigg	42	37	27	18	13	3								
Greenhead	49	44	34	24	19	10	7							
Gilsland	51	46	36	26	21	12	9	2						
Walton	58	53	43	33	29	20	17	10	8					
Newtown	60	55	45	35	30	22	19	12	10	2				
Crosby	65	60	50	40	36	27	24	17	15	7	5			
Carlisle	70	65	55	45	40	32	29	22	20	12	10	5		
Burgh-by-Sands	77	72	62	52	47	38	36	29	27	19	17	12	7	
Bowness	84	79	69	59	55	46	44	37	35	27	25	20	15	8

Distance Calculator (kilometers)

	Wallsend	Tyne bridge	Heddon	A68 Errington Arms	Chollerford	Housesteads	Steel Rigg	Greenhead	Gilsland	Walton	Newtown	Crosby	Carlisle	Burgh by Sands	Bowness
Wallsend															
Tyne bridge	8														
Heddon	24	16													
A68 Errington Arms	40	32	16												
Chollerford	48	40	24	8											
Housesteads	63	55	39	24	16										
Steel Rigg	67	59	43	29	21	5									
Greenhead	79	71	55	39	31	16	11								
Gilsland	82	74	58	42	34	20	15	3							
Walton	93	85	69	53	47	32	27	16	13						
Newtown	96	88	72	56	46	35	30	19	16	3					
Crosby	104	96	80	64	58	43	39	27	24	12	8				
Carlisle	112	104	88	72	64	51	46	35	32	19	16	8			
Burgh-by-Sands	123	115	99	83	75	61	58	46	43	30	27	19	11		
Bowness	135	126	110	94	88	74	70	59	56	43	40	32	24	13	

Of all the National Trails and long-distance routes in Britain, Hadrian's Wall Path must rank as one of the easiest to get to. It is served by two regional cities, Carlisle (in the west) and Newcastle upon Tyne (to the east), both of which have inter-city rail links and National Express coach services. Newcastle itself has its own regional airport with scheduled services to many UK and overseas destinations.

Once you have arrived, moving between the two main centres along the Trail is relatively straight forward. Timing is important and you must plan ahead. Don't assume that buses will serve every access point to the Trail because you will be disappointed. Please bear in mind that the frequency of service, and sometimes the service itself, varies according to the time of year. **The AD 122 Hadrian's Wall bus** service, for example, operates a daily service between 29th May and 26th September, connecting the Trail to the main towns and villages where most of the B&B accommodation is to be found. Outside of this season you will find it more difficult to plan your itinerary.

Arriving in Newcastle:

By air

Newcastle airport couldn't be more convenient for the start of your holiday. You are quickly through baggage reclaim and passport control and onto the Tyne and Wear Metro which has its own airport station. The Metro is a modern, frequent and reliable service but the stations are not staffed and tickets are purchased from a machine. Not every Metro station has a change machine so a **top tip** is to have change ready. In January 2004 a single fare from the airport to the Central Station was £2.20 and the journey takes about 25 minutes.

By ferry

For anyone arriving from Holland or Scandinavia the way to the National Trail from the Royal Quays ferry terminal is very straightforward. To go into Newcastle take the special 327 ferry bus direct to Central Station. The station is a useful hub to orientate yourself around Newcastle with the city's youth hostel, for example, only three stops away where you should alight at Jesmond Metro.

To go to the start of the National Trail at Wallsend you will need to first take a local bus service (333) for the 10 minute journey to North Shields town centre, and then take the Metro (have change ready) to Wallsend Metro station.

By train

This couldn't be easier. Newcastle is served by the East Coast Main Line with frequent GNER services from London King's Cross, Edinburgh and Glasgow. For telephone bookings: 08457 225 225. www.gner.co.uk

Virgin Cross Country also connects Newcastle with Edinburgh, the south coast of England, and Wales. For telephone bookings: 08457 222 333. www.virgin.com/trains

Another important regional service into Newcastle is by First Trains with its Trans Pennine Express service from Liverpool, Manchester and Leeds. www.firstgroup.com/tpexpress

Arriving in Carlisle:

By train

Carlisle is served by the West Coast Main Line with frequent Virgin Trains from Glasgow, London Euston and the south. Contact details as above.

Coach travel

National Express Coaches serve both Newcastle (St James' Boulevard - five minutes walk from Central Station) and Carlisle (bus station in Lonsdale Street). For telephone bookings: 08705 808080. www.nationalexpress.com

Leaving Newcastle:

By ferry

To return to the Royal Quays ferry terminal take the 327 ferry bus that leaves outside Central Station only. The frequency depends upon the company that you are sailing with. For DFDS it leaves $2^{1}/_{2}$ and $1^{1}/_{4}$ hours before the boat sails. For Fjiordline it leaves $2^{1}/_{2}$ and $1^{1}/_{2}$ hours before the boat sails.

Traveline

The national public transport information line is 0870 608 2 608 or visit: www.traveline.org.uk

National Rail enquiries

National Rail enquiry service: 08457 484950
or visit www.nationalrail.co.uk

Travelling around the World Heritage Site

The following is a guide only to the main public transport services that you are likely to use within and around Hadrian's Wall World Heritage Site. The Hadrian's Wall Information Line will send you the 2004 public transport guide that summarises the timetables for the services listed. (haltwhistletic@btconnect.com or telephone 01434 322002)

AD 122 Hadrian's Wall bus

The route, with other interim stops, connects Wallsend with Newcastle; Heddon-on-the-Wall; Errington Arms (A68); Corbridge; Hexham; Chesters Roman Fort, Chollerford; Housesteads Roman Fort; Once Brewed National Park Visitor Centre; Vindolanda Roman Fort; Milecastle Inn near Cawfields; Roman Army Museum at Walltown; Greenhead; Gilsland; Birdoswald Roman Fort; Lanercost Priory; Brampton; Crosby-on-Eden; Carlisle; Kirkandrews; Beaumont; Burgh by Sands; Drumburgh; Glasson; Port Carlisle and Bowness-on-Solway.

685 bus service between Carlisle and Newcastle

Connects Newcastle with Heddon; Corbridge; Hexham; Haydon Bridge; Haltwhistle; Greenhead; Brampton and Carlisle.

93 bus service between Carlisle and Bowness-on-Solway

An important local service for getting in and out of Bowness. A top tip would be to request the full timetable from either Traveline or the Hadrian's Wall Information Line. The service connects Carlisle with Beaumont; Burgh-by-Sands; Dykesfield; Drumburgh; Glasson; Port Carlisle and Bowness-on-Solway.

880 bus service between Hexham, Wark and Bellingham

Useful if you want to travel between Hexham; Acomb (for the youth hostel); Wall; Chollerford; Humshaugh and Bellingham.

185 bus service between Carlisle and Housesteads Roman Fort

Connects Carlisle with Brampton; Gilsland; Roman Army Museum at Walltown; Haltwhistle; Once Brewed National Park Visitor Centre and Housesteads Roman Fort.

Tyne Valley Railway Line

Regular trains connect Newcastle with Wylam; Prudhoe; Corbridge; Hexham; Bardon Mill; Haydon Bridge; Haltwhistle; Brampton and Carlisle. (Not every station is served by every service).

Other services

94, 97 bus services out of Carlisle:

With careful planning it is possible to get to or from Walton or Newtown using this bus service. Request a timetable from Traveline.

Taxis

Go to www.traintaxi.co.uk for details of taxi services available from the railway stations between Tyneside and Carlisle. Traintaxi lists all the train, metro, tram and underground stations in Britain and lists up to three local taxi or minicab firms serving each station.

Secure car parking

If you arrive by car you will want to leave it somewhere that is as safe as possible. Sometimes hotels will oblige but if you need to use a car park you will generally find it easier to find space in Newcastle where there is more capacity. In any case it is advisable to pre-book. Please also make a special note that there is absolutely nowhere for day visitors to park in Bowness-on-Solway. (See below for long-stay parking in Bowness). The following places have been recommended.

Newcastle airport

You don't have to travel by air to use the airport's secure long-stay car parking facility. The airport is easily accessed from the A1, and the Metro journey into Newcastle city centre takes only 25 minutes. A week's car park charge is around £34 although there are often discounted offers which can be arranged through Co-op Travelcare. Contact the Prudhoe branch for the latest deals, telephone 01661 836800.

Royal Quays ferry terminal

If arriving by ferry there is a long-stay secure car park at the ferry terminal, ask your travel agent for details.

Carlisle railway station

You can leave your car at the station for up to five days; the current charge is £5 per day, payable at the meter.

Carlisle, Secor Indoor Garage, Viaduct Estate

The cost for one day plus overnight is currently £7; for a week the basic cost is £25. Telephone 0776 342 3030 for full details.

Bowness-on-Solway

Parking on private property by arrangement.
Telephone 016973 51788.

Tide times for the Solway coast

The Solway coast between Dykesfield and Drumburgh and also between Port Carlisle and Bowness-on-Solway is at sea level. These sites can be affected by tidal flooding. You must be aware of when this is likely to occur and allow sufficient time for a safe walk along these sections. Information is provided for your benefit in several ways.

Hadrian's Wall Newsletter - This is published three times a year by the English Heritage World Heritage Site Co-ordination Unit, copies of which should be available from the main Tourist Information Centres, also those B&Bs that subscribe to the magazine. Each edition includes the tide prediction tables, together with instructions on how to interpret them, for the next four months.

Accommodation providers - A complete set of tide tables for 2004 is issued to those accommodation providers who have paid for an entry in the 2004 Accommodation Guide.

Notice boards - Located at Dykesfield and Bowness-on-Solway. The boards contain the current month's tide prediction tables.

The Internet - The UK Hydrographic Office provides a free seven day prediction service and you can access it any time by going to www.ukho.gov.uk then proceed as follows:

select: Easy Tide

select: Europe and Northern Waters and Mediterranean

select: England

select: Silloth

select: Predict

You will then see a seven day tide prediction forecast table. You are interested in the high tide (times and heights of 9 metres and above) because this is when the affected parts of the Trail may flood.

However, because the prediction is for the nearest port of Silloth you will need to do a conversion for the Trail as follows:

1. During Greenwich Mean Time (also known as winter time) add on one hour.
2. During British Summer Time add on two hours.

You will now have a time for high tide adjusted for the Trail. **Finally, allow for an hour either side of high tide when the sections affected should be avoided.**

Do bear in mind that the tide tables give predictions only and that many conditions, for example wind speed and atmospheric pressure, can influence the likelihood of the Solway marshes flooding. The Solway estuary can look an entirely benign place, but the water can rise very quickly.

Tourist Information Centres (TICs)

Tyneside and Northumberland

128 Grainger Street, Newcastle upon Tyne, NE1 5AF.
Telephone: 0191 277 8000.

Central Station, Main Concourse, Newcastle upon Tyne, NE1 5DL.
Telephone: 0191 277 8000.

Hill Street, Corbridge, Northumberland NE45 5AA.*
Telephone: 01434 632815.

Wentworth Car Park, Hexham, Northumberland NE46 1XD.
Telephone: 01434 652200.

Once Brewed. Northumberland National Park Visitor Centre, Military Road, Bardon Mill, Hexham, Northumberland NE47 7AN.
Telephone: 01434 344396.

Haltwhistle. Railway Station, Station Road, Haltwhistle, Northumberland. NE49 9HN. Telephone: 01434 322002. Haltwhistle TIC is also the Hadrian's Wall Information Line.

Cumbria

The Moot Hall, Market Place, Brampton, Cumbria CA8 1RW.
Telephone: 01697 73433.*

Old Town Hall, Green Market, Carlisle, Cumbria CA3 8JE. Telephone: 01228 625600.

* Open April to October only.

The 24 hour NHS Direct telephone help-line is 0845 4647. The service is staffed by nurses and you can call for immediate advice if you or a family member feels ill. Your accommodation address should also be able to advise you of local GP and dentist surgeries.

Hospitals close to Hadrian's Wall:

Emergencies
In an emergency dial 999 or 112.

Newcastle General Hospital,
Westgate Road, Newcastle upon Tyne.
Telephone: 0191 273 8811.

Hexham General Hospital,
Corbridge Road, Hexham.
Telephone: 01434 655655.

Haltwhistle War Memorial Hospital,
Westgate, Haltwhistle.
Telephone: 01434 320225. 24-hour, minor injuries only.

Brampton War Memorial Hospital,
Tree Road, Brampton.
Telephone: 016977 2534.
Open only 08.00 to 20.00. Minor injuries only.

Carlisle Infirmary Hospital,
Newtown Road, Carlisle.
Telephone: 01228 523444.

Pharmacies
The following are the pharmacies that we consider to be the most useful for walkers:

Wallsend

Boots Chemist. The Forum. Telephone: 0191 262 3673. Open: Mon - Sat 09.00 to 17.30.

Newcastle

Boots Chemist (next to Greys Monument, top of Grey Street). Telephone; 0191 232 4423. Open: Mon - Sat: 08.00 to 18.00; to 19.00 Thurs.

Wylam

Wylam Pharmacy, Main Road. Telephone: 01661 852253. Open: Mon - Fri: 08.30 to 18.00. Sat: 08.30 to 13.00.

Corbridge

Henderson's Pharmacy. Town Hall Building, Princes Street. Telephone: 01434 632046. Open: Mon - Fri: 09.00 to 18.00. Sat: 09.00 to 16.00.

Hexham

Pattinson's Pharmacy, Fore Street. Telephone: 01434 603080. Open: Mon, Tues, Wed, Fri: 08.45 to 17.15. Thurs, Sat: 08.45 to 17.00.

Haltwhistle

Moss Pharmacy, Eden House, Westgate. Telephone 01434 320511. Open: Mon - Fri: 09.00 to 18.00. Sat: 09.00 to 13.00.

Brampton

H. Jobson, Market Place. Telephone: 016977 2501. Open: Mon, Wed, Fri: 09.00 to 18.30. Tues: 09.00 to 17.30. Thurs, Sat: 09.00 to 17.00.

Carlisle

Boots Chemist, 43 English Street. Telephone: 01228 542944. Open: Mon - Sat 08.45 to 17.30.

Historic sites, museums and visitor centres ●

This list includes the Roman sites and museums, other historic sites, attractions and visitor centres close to the Trail. Where helpful OS Grid References are given, otherwise distance or brief directions from the Trail. For full details refer to the relevant web sites or organisation membership handbooks. There are, of course, many other attractions in places like Newcastle, your suggestions for next year's guide are welcome. The tourist information centres are listed separately.

Tyneside and Northumberland

South Shields

Arbeia Roman Fort. Telephone 0191 456 1369. Not on the Trail but well worth a visit. 15 minutes walk from South Shields Metro. Site free but £1.50 entry to award winning Time Quest - hands on archaeology display. Open: Easter to Sept, Mon - Sat 10.00 to 17.30; Sun 13.00 to 17.00. From Oct to Easter, Mon-Sat 10.00 to 16.00. Closed Sunday. Time Quest hours vary, please check. www.twmuseums.org.uk

Wallsend

Segedunum Roman Fort - Bathhouse and Museum. Telephone 0191 236 9347. Five minutes walk from Wallsend Metro. At the beginning/ end of route. Passport stamping point. Admission charge, reduction for English Heritage members, please call site for details. Open daily, April - Oct 10.00 to 17.00. Nov - March 10.00 to 15.30. (Also café and permissive water tap, ask for permission at reception desk - see relevant lists). www.twmuseums.org.uk

Gateshead

Baltic Centre for Contemporary Art. Telephone 0191 478 1810. On the Gateshead side of the Gateshead Millennium Bridge. Free admission. Open: Mon - Wed 10.00 to 19.00; Thurs 10.00 to 22.00; Sun 10.00 to 17.00. Also café and restaurant. www.balticmill.com

Newcastle

Bessie Surtees House. Telephone 0191 269 1200. Free admission. 50 metres from Trail, walk away from the River Tyne at the Swing Bridge, into Sandhill. Open: Mon to Fri, 10.00 to 16.00 except Bank Holidays. www.english-heritage.org.uk

Castle Keep, Castle Garth. Telephone 0191 478 1810. Newcastle's Norman Keep, five minutes' walk from the Tyne bridge. Open: April - Sept 09.30 to 17.30. Oct - March 09.30 to 16.30. www.castlekeep-newcastle.org.uk

Museum of Antiquities. Telephone 0191 222 7849. (Located in the University of Newcastle campus, nearest Metro station Haymarket. Free. Open: Mon to Sat 10.00 to 17.00. Sun closed. www.ncl.ac.uk/antiquities

Newburn

Tyne Riverside Country Park. Visitor centre. Free. Telephone 0191 281 0973. 100 metres from Trail, visible from the boat launching slipway. Visitor centre is usually open on Sat & Sun 13.00 to 17.00. Open other times depending on availability of staff. WC and water available daily (see page 42): 09.00 to 17.00.

Wylam

George Stephenson's Birthplace Cottage. Admission charge, National Trust members free. GR: NZ 126 650. Approx 0.5 mile (0.8 km) west of Trail. Open: 1st April to the 1st November, Thurs - Sun, 13.00 to 17.00. The tea room is open 12.00 to 17.00. www.nationaltrust.org.uk

Corbridge

Corbridge Roman Fort. Telephone 01434 632349. Admission charge, English Heritage members free. Signed from the town centre. Open: April - Sept 10.00 to 18.00. Oct 10.00 to 16.00. Nov - March, weekends only 10.00 to 16.00. www.english-heritage.org.uk

Aydon Castle. Telephone 01434 632450. Admission charge, English Heritage members free. GR: NZ 002 663. One mile (1.6 km) north east of Corbridge. Open: April - Sept 10.00 to 18.00. www.english-heritage.org.uk

Chollerford

Chesters Roman Fort. Telephone 01434 681379. Passport stamping point. Admission charge, English Heritage members free. On Trail. Open: April - Sept 09.30 to 18.00. Oct to March 10.00 to 16.00. Also water tap, permissive WC, café. (See relevant lists). www.english-heritage.org.uk

Housesteads

Housesteads Roman Fort. Telephone 01434 344363. Admission charge, English Heritage and National Trust members free. On Trail. Open: April - Sept 10.00 to 18.00. Oct - March 10.00 to 16.00. Also refreshment kiosk and watering point 0.5 mile (0.8 km) away at car park - see relevant lists). www.english-heritage.org.uk

Once Brewed

Once Brewed Visitor Centre. Telephone 01434 344396. Free. GR NY 752 669. 0.5 mile (0.8 km) from Trail which is accessed at Steel Rigg car park. Also WC, drinks vending machine and water tap. (See relevant lists).

Vindolanda Roman Fort. Telephone 01434 344 277. Admission charge. GR: NY: 770664. Open: April - Sept 10.00 to 18.00. Oct - mid Nov 10.00 to 17.00. www.vindolanda.com

Walltown

Carvoran Roman Army Museum. Telephone 016977 47485. Admission charge. 3 minutes walk from route, from Trail turn left out of Walltown car park. Open: April - Sept 10.00 to 18.00. Oct to mid Nov 10.00 to 17.00. Café for paying customers only. www.vindolanda.com

Cumbria

Gilsland

Birdoswald Roman Fort. Telephone 016977 47602. Admission charge. On Trail. Open: 1 March - 9 November 10.00 to 17.30 daily (last admission 17.00). Café open: 10.00 to 17.00. Also passport stamping point, permissive WC and water tap, see relevant lists). Internet facility. www.birdoswaldromanfort.org

Lanercost

Lanercost Priory. Telephone 01697 73030. Admission charge, English Heritage members free. GR: NY 513 299. 1 mile (1.6 km) from Trail. Open: April - Sept 10.00 to 18.00. Oct 10.00 to 16.00 Thurs to Mon (closed Tues and Wed). Closed Nov - March. www.english-heritage.org.uk

Carlisle

Tullie House Museum. Telephone 01228 534781. Admission charge. Five minutes walk from Trail. Open: April - June & Sept - Oct, Mon - Sat 10.00 to 17.00; Sun 12.00 to 17.00. July & Aug hours as above except Sun 11.00 to 17.00. Oct - March, Mon - Sat 10.00 to 16.00; Sun 12.00 to 16.00. Also café. www.tulliehouse.co.uk

Youth hostels

There are four permanent plus two seasonal youth hostels handy for the National Trail. The following list is for guidance only, for full details refer to the 2004 YHA accommodation guide. www.yha.org.uk

Tyneside and Northumberland

Newcastle upon Tyne: 107 Jesmond Road Newcastle upon Tyne, Tyne and Wear, NE2 1NJ. E- mail: newcastle@yha.org.uk Tel: 0870 770 5972 Fax: 0870 770 5973. **Internet facility**. Grid ref: NZ 257 656. Nearest Metro station: Jesmond.

Acomb: Main Street, Acomb, Hexham, Northumberland, NE46 4PL. Tel: 0870 770 5664. Grid ref: NY 934 666.

Once Brewed: Military Road, Bardon Mill, Northumberland, NE47 7AN. E-mail: oncebrewed@yha.org.uk Tel: 0870 770 5980 Fax: 0870 770 5981. **Internet facility**. Grid ref: NY 752 668.

Greenhead: Greenhead, Brampton, Cumbria, CA8 7HG. E-mail: greenhead@yha.org.uk Tel: 0870 770 5842 Fax: 0870 770 5843. Grid ref: NY 659 655.

Cumbria

Birdoswald (seasonal): Located within Birdoswald Roman Fort, Gilsland. Tel: 0870 770 6124. Grid ref: NY 615 663.

Carlisle (seasonal): Old Brewery Residences, Bridge Lane, Caldewgate, Carlisle, Cumbria. CA2 5SR E-mail: dee.carruthers@unn.ac.uk Tel: 0870 770 5752 Fax : 0870 770 5752. Grid ref: NY 394 560.

Camping sites, barns and private hostels

We strongly recommend that you obtain a copy of the 2004 Accommodation Guide (see page 16) which contains full details of the amenities and services available at the camping sites listed in the guide. However, not all of the sites on or close to the Trail are in this year's guide so, as a service to you the walker, we have decided to list here every inspected site, plus those other non-inspected places which sometimes take in campers. **For these non-accredited sites no claim can be made as to their quality standards.**

We do advise that you **book in advance** because some of the sites listed are relatively small.

Northumberland

Heddon-on-the-Wall

Heddon View, Birkes Road, East Heddon (camping). Home Telephone: 0191 267 1116. Grid ref: NZ 146 680. Contact: Gillian Brow. Facilities: Use of farmhouse tap and bathroom. Able to pick up and drop off at Heddon or Newburn. Please make arrangements beforehand. Enquiries can also be made at the Visitors' Centre at Tyne Riverside Country Park, Newburn. Telephone: 0191 264 8501. **Non-accredited site.**

Harlow Hill

Belvedere campsite. Telephone 01661 853689. Grid ref: NZ 079 683. Open all year. (Also permissive water tap, please ask for permission in garage).

Well House Farm Camping & Caravanning. Contact: Kenneth Richardson. Telephone: 01661 842193. Grid ref: NZ 043 666. Distance from Trail: 1.5 miles (2.4 km). Open: Mar - Oct.

Acomb

Fallowfield Dene Caravan & Camping, Acomb. Contact: Dennis and Jenny Burnell. Telephone: 01434 603553. Four star site. Distance from Trail: 2 miles (3.2 km). Grid ref: NY 938 676. Open: 19th March to 2/1/05.

Wall

Wall village green. One night's free camping courtesy of Wall parish council. Public WC on site. Distance from Trail: 0.2 miles (0.4 km). Grid ref: NY 928 693. **Non-accredited site.**

Walwick

Green Carts Farm (camping). Telephone 01434 681320. Contact Sandra Maughan. Grid ref: NY 887 717. **Non-accredited site**. 0.5 km from Trail. Open April until the autumn.

Northumberland National Park

Old Repeater Station (hostel). Telephone 01434 688668/07941 238641. Grid ref: NY 816 701. 0.5 mile (0.8 km) from the Trail. Dormitory accommodation. Opening end of May to end of year. Please telephone for directions.

Hadrian Lodge (hostel). Telephone 01434 684867. Grid ref: NY 832 666. 1.8 miles (2.8 km) from Trail. Open all year.

Holmhead (camping barn). Telephone 016977 47402. Grid ref: NY 662 671. On the Trail. Open except Christmas and new year.

Winshields Farm Camping & Caravans. Telephone: 01434 344243. Distance from Trail 0.5 miles (0.8 km). Grid ref: NY 745 669. Open: April - Oct.

Hadrian's Wall Caravan and Camping Site. Contact: Graham Read. Telephone 01434 320495. Three star site. Distance from Trail: 1 mile (1.6 km). Grid ref: NY 730 658. Pick-up and drop-off service by prior arrangement.

Greenhead

Roam 'n' Rest Caravan Park, Greenhead (camping). Contact: Joan Waugh. Telephone 016977 47213. Three star site. Grid ref: NY 655 654. Distance from Trail 0.5 miles (0.8 km). Open: March - Oct.

Cumbria campsites/camping barns

Banks

Banks Head Camping Barn. For information telephone 016977 3198; for bookings telephone YHA booking line 0870 770 6113. On the Trail. Grid ref: NY 579 649. Open: all year.

Laversdale

The Sportsman Inn. Telephone 01228 573255. Refer list of pubs for other details. **Non accredited** camping at rear. Approx one mile (1.6 km) from GR 488 618 - link signed as a bridle way.

Green Acres Caravan Park (camping). Telephone 01228 675418. Grid ref: NY 419 615. Distance from Trail 2.5 miles. Open: April - Oct.

Dandy Dinmont Caravan Park (camping). Telephone 01228 674611. Contact Barbara Inglis. Grid ref: NY 396 619. Distance from Trail 3.5 miles. Open: March to Oct.

Grinsdale

West View Camping and Caravan site. Telephone 01228 526336. Contact John Edgar. Distance from Trail 0.5 miles. Grid ref: NY 365 572. Open: Mar to middle of Oct.

Port Carlisle

Glendale Caravan Park. Telephone 016973 51317. Accredited caravan site but **non-accredited** camping site, please telephone for details. Grid ref: NY 244 612. Five minutes walk from Trail. Open: all year.

Port Carlisle

Kirkland House. Telephone 016973 51400. Contact Daphne Hogg. This camping barn is likely to open about June, please telephone for details.

Bowness-on-Solway

Bowness village hall. Telephone 016973 51322. By arrangement, groups can book the hall for basic sleeping amenities.

Obtaining cash & paying for things

Too many times in 2003 B&B owners ended up driving walkers to the nearest cash-point machine because their guests were ill-prepared for the fact that, apart from the larger hotels, very few small businesses accept payments by debit or credit cards. With just a little planning this needn't happen. Together, the available cash-point machines and Post Offices (where the you can draw out cash if you bank with Alliance and Leicester, Barclays, Cahoot, Co-op; Lloyds TSB or Smile) offer ample places to obtain money. Pay particular attention to the opening times of the small Post Offices.

Shops

A handful of shops (refer list of shops) also allow payment by debit/credit card and some also have the cash-back facility. (See the list of shops for details). To pay by using this method your card must have the MAESTRO symbol on it.

Cashing travellers' cheques

This will be of interest to our guests from overseas. Banks will, of course, cash travellers' cheques, but you can also cash them at the main post offices in Carlisle and Newcastle. The small post offices will not cash travellers' cheques.

Using cash-point machines if you are from overseas

You may use your bank ATM card in most UK bank cash-point machines if your card has the CIRRUS symbol on it.

Bureau de Change

There is a Bureau de Change in the Royal Quays ferry terminal that is open for the arrival of every ferry from Holland and Scandinavia. The main banks in Newcastle will also exchange foreign currency. A walker's recommendation in 2003 was to check the Bureau de Change in Marks and Spencer, in Northumberland Street, Newcastle, which in 2003 reportedly gave a very good rate of exchange for currency and travellers' cheques.

Cash-point machines

This list is necessarily selective, it includes those cash-point machines that we think will be most useful to you. Some are in the towns and villages close by where walkers typically find B&Bs. (We do welcome suggestions for machines that you think should be in next year's guide). Bank opening hours are also shown. All banks have a cash-point machine unless otherwise stated.

Tyneside and Northumberland

Wallsend

Co-op Bank. The Forum shopping centre. Five minutes walk from Segedunum; from the site walk up Station Road to the traffic lights, the Forum is across the road to your left.

The following cash-point machines and banks are in High Street West. Directions as above to the traffic lights. Turn left for:

Lloyds TSB. Open: Mon - Fri 09.30 to 16.30; Wed from 10.00.

Barclays. Open: Mon - Fri 09.00 to 17.00; Wed from 10.00; Sat 10.00 to 14.00.

Turn right for:

Halifax & Nationwide cash-point machines.

Lloyds TSB (yes, another!). Open: Mon - Fri 09.00 to 17.00; Wed from 10.00; Sat 09.00 to 13.00.

Newcastle

Central station has three cash-point machines located next to the confectionery shop, approaching platform 2. The machines belong to Nat West; Abbey National and Royal Bank of Scotland. To obtain money while walking the Trail in Newcastle we suggest that, using the Tyne Bridge as a landmark, you walk up Dean Street which leads into Grey Street where you will find banks and cash-point machines very close to each other and in the following order:

Royal Bank of Scotland. Open: Mon - Fri 09.15 to 16.45. (Opens 10.00 on Wed).

Bank of Scotland. Open: Mon - Fri 09.00 to 17.00. (Opens 10.00 on Wed).

Barclays. Market Street (just off Grey Street). Open: Mon - Fri 09.00 to 17.00 (Opens 10.00 on Wed), Sat 10.00 - 16.00.

Lloyds TSB. Open: Mon - Fri 09.00 to 17.00 (Opens 10.00 on Tues), Sat 9.30 to 12.30.

Nat West. Open: Mon - Fri 09.00 to 17.00. (Opens 9.30 on Wed).

HSBC (beside Grey's Monument). Open: Mon, Tues, Wed, Fri 09.00 to 17.00. Thurs 09.00 to 18.00. Sat 10.00 to 14.30. (It is only 10 minutes walk from the Tyne bridge to Grey's monument, the centre of Newcastle's shopping district).

Newburn

Lloyds TSB, Station Road. Open: Mon - Fri 09.30 to 16.30. (Opens 10.00 on Wed).

Barclays, Station Road. No cash-point machine, open: Mon - Fri 09.30 to 16.30. (Opens 10.00 on Wed).

Heddon-on-the-Wall

Spar Supermarket and Shell garage. Telephone 01661 852276. Open: Mon - Sat 07.00 to 21.00; Sun 08.00 to 20.00. Cash-point machine inside shop (UK banks only) for which a charge is made; permissive WC & water tap outside (see relevant lists).

Corbridge

Barclays. Market Place. Open: Mon - Fri 09.30 to 16.00. (Opens 10.00 Wed).

Lloyds TSB. Middle Street. No cash-point machine. Open: Mon - Fri 09.30 to 13.00.

Hexham

HSBC. Fore Street. Open: Mon - Fri 09.30 to 16.30.

Barclays. Priestpopple. Open: Mon - Fri 09.00 to 17.00. (Opens 10.00 on Wed). Sat 10 to 2.

Lloyds TSB. Cattle Market. Open: Mon - Fri 09.00 to 17.00 (Opens 10.00 on Tues), Sat 9.30 to 12.30.

Nat West Battle Hill. Open: Mon - Fri 09.00 to 16.30. (Opens 9.30 on Wed).

Haltwhistle

HSBC. Market square. Open: Mon - Fri 09.30 to 16.30.

Barclays Westgate. Open: Mon - Fri 09.30 to 16.30. (Opens 10.00 Wed).

Cumbria

Brampton

HSBC. Front Street. Open: Mon - Fri 09.30 to 16.30.

Barclays. Open: Mon - Fri 09.30 to 16.30. (Opens 10.00 on Wed).

Carlisle

HSBC. English Street. Open: Mon - Fri 09.30 to 17.00, Sat 09.30 to 12.30.

Barclays. English Street. Open: Mon - Sat 09.00 to 17.00. (Opens 10.00 on Wed). Sat 09.00 to 13.00.

Clydesdale. English Street. Open: Mon - Fri 09.15 to 16.45. (Opens 09.45 on Wed).

Nat West. English Street. Open: Mon - Fri 09.00 to 16.30. (Opens 09.30 on Wed). Sat 09.30 to 13.30.

Northern Rock. Devonshire Street. Open: Mon - Fri 09.00 to 17.00. (Opens 09.30 Tues). Sat 09.00 to 12.00.

Finding somewhere to fill your water bottles on a hot sunny day can, if you are unlucky, occupy your mind to the point of distraction. We have done our best to prepare a list of places where you can replenish your supplies without recourse to knocking on doors, which in any case is not encouraged.

There is now a string of water taps that we will hopefully continue to add to over time, as well as other places, granted on a permissive basis, where owners have kindly agreed to let you call for water. Please respect the goodwill that many folk have shown. Three churches have offered the use of their outdoor water taps - please consider leaving them a small donation in appreciation.

For all sites the taps are advertised as a summer only amenity.

We hope by the summer to have additional sites in Northumberland, courtesy of Northumbria Water. Check the National Trail website before you set out (www.nationaltrail.co.uk/hadrianswall). They will, of course, be in next year's guide.

Tyneside and Northumberland

Segedunum Roman Fort. See opening times in list of historic sites, museums and visitor centres. Permissive water tap, ask at the reception desk. (Also café, WCs, see other lists).

St Peter's Marina Office (Indoor tap & WC): Telephone: 0191 265 4472. Available daily 09.00 to 17.00. (Location: St Peter's Basin, east side of bridge, directly on the Trail). Please note that this is a permissive water tap, courtesy of the Marina owners.

Newburn Sports Centre. Five minutes walk from the Trail at Newburn. From the boat launching slipway walk towards the visitor centre, turn right, pass the Keelman Inn, the sports centre is a tall modern brick building about 100 metres past the Keelman. Open: Mon - Fri 09.00 to 22.00. Sat & Sun: 09.00 to 17.00. Permissive water tap, ask at the reception desk. Cold drinks and confectionary vending machines. Walkers can use the showers for 75p.

Newburn. Tyne Riverside Country Park Visitor Centre. Visible from the boat launching slipway. Water available from the WC which is open daily 09.00 to 17.00.

Heddon-on-the-Wall, Spar supermarket & Shell garage. Permissive water tap. (Also WC, general store, cash machine, see relevant lists).

Belvedere campsite, Harlow Hill. Grid ref: NZ 079 683. On the Trail. Permissive water tap. Tap inside the campsite. Ask for permission at garage next door.

Whittledene reservoirs. 0.6 mile (1 km) west of Harlow Hill, to the south of the B6318. Situated at Grid ref: NZ 065 680 at the Northumbria Water site, part of the fishing club. Permissive water tap, also WC, both amenities sponsored by Northumbrian Water.

Chesters Roman Fort, Chollerford. Signed from the B6318, the Trail passes the site entrance. English Heritage have kindly agreed to plumb in an outside water tap, situated to the left of the shop entrance. Available any time. (Also WC, café, see relevant lists). See site opening times in list of historic sites, museums and visitor centres.

Housesteads Roman Fort. Located in the car park close to the shop entrance. It is approx 0.5 mile (0.8 km) from the Trail at the bottom of the hill. Available any time. (Also WC, refreshments, see WC and café lists).

Once Brewed Visitor Centre. Approx 0.5 mile (0.8 km) from the Trail, leave the route at Steel Rigg car park. Located in the Visitor Centre car park near the pay and display ticket machine. Available any time. (Also WC, internet facility and drinks vending machine, see lists).

Cawfields Quarry car park. On the Trail. Located on the toilet block wall, available any time.

Greenhead Youth Hostel. Grid ref: NY 660 654. 0.5 km south of the Trail in Greenhead village. The YHA have very kindly agreed to allow walkers to use the water supply in the hostel during the summer season. It will be available during most daytime hours although the YHA reserves the right to close the hostel at any time.

Cumbria

Birdoswald Roman Fort. On the Trail, also a passport stamping station, located in the site's courtyard. Permissive water tap, ask at reception. (Also WC, café, internet facility, see other lists).

Sands Sports Centre, Carlisle. On the Trail, also a passport stamping station. Permissive water tap, ask at reception. Available normal opening hours, see page 57. (Also cafe, WC, see other lists).

Beaumont - St Mary's Churchyard. On the Trail. Walk clockwise around the church to find the tap in a wooden cupboard. Permissive water tap.

Drumburgh, The Grange farm. Permissive water tap and WC, also drinks vending machine (see relevant lists). Located up cul-de-sac opposite junction in village, from where it will be signed. Open: 08.00 to 17.00, other times by arrangement.

Port Carlisle, Solway Methodist Church. On the Trail. A quiet place for retreat. Permissive WC and water tap available. Open: May - Aug from morning to early evening.

Port Carlisle Bowling Club. Next to the trail. Permissive water tap. Tap attached to the front of the bowling clubhouse.

Bowness-on-Solway. Located in St Michael's Churchyard, two minutes walk from the Trail. Walk clockwise around the church to find the permissive water tap.

Tyneside and Northumberland

Segedunum Roman Fort. Telephone 0191 295 5757. Five minutes walk from Wallsend Metro. Permissive WC (and water tap), ask at reception desk. Also Passport stamping point. See list of historic sites for opening etc. times.

St Peter's Marina Office. Telephone: 0191 265 4472. Available Mon - Sun 09.00 to 17.00. (Location: St Peter's Basin, east side of bascule bridge over marina entrance, on the Trail). Permissive WC, call at office.

Newcastle Quayside. East end of Swing Bridge, public WC, 20p coin in slot.

Newburn. Tyne Riverside Country Park Visitor Centre. One minutes walk from the boat launching slipway. Water is also available from the WC which is open daily 09.00 to 17.00.

Newburn Sports Centre. Five minutes walk from the Trail at Newburn. From the boat launching slipway walk towards the Visitor Centre, turn right towards the Keelman Inn. The sports centre is a tall modern brick building about 150 metres from the Keelman. Open: Mon - Fri 09.00 to 22.00; Sat & Sun 09.00 to 17.00. Also permissive water tap, ask at the reception desk. Cold drinks and confectionary vending machines. Walkers can use the showers for 75p.

Heddon-on-the-Wall, Spar supermarket & Shell garage. Permissive WC. (Also water tap, general store, cash machine (see relevant lists).

Whittledene reservoirs. 0.6 mile (1 km) west of Harlow Hill, to the south of the B6318. Situated at GR 065 680 at the Northumbria Water site, part of the fishing club facilities. Also permissive watering point, both amenities sponsored by Northumbrian Water.

Chesters Roman Fort, Chollerford. Signed from the B6318, the Trail passes in front of site entrance. Permissive WC, ask at reception desk. English Heritage have agreed to let genuine Trail walkers use the site WC - but please consider purchasing something from the shop if you are not visiting the site. (Note free admission to English Heritage members). (Also, café on site, see relevant lists for opening etc. times).

Housesteads Roman Fort. Located in the car park close to the shop entrance, approx 0.5 mile (0.8 km) from the Trail at the bottom of the hill. Closed at night. Also refreshments, see list of cafés.

Once Brewed Visitor Centre. Approx 0.5 mile (0.8 km) from the Trail, leave the route at Steel Rigg car park. Located next to the information centre. (Also water and drinks vending machine, see relevant lists).

Cawfields Quarry car park. On the Trail route, available any time. (Also water tap - see relevant list for details).

Walltown Quarry car park. On the Trail route, available any time.

Greenhead Youth Hostel. Grid ref: NY 660 654. 0.5 km south of the Trail in Greenhead village. The YHA have very kindly agreed to allow walkers to use the WC in the hostel during the summer season. It will be available during most daytime hours although the YHA reserves the right to close the hostel at any time.

Cumbria

Gilsland. Public WC, five minutes walk from the Trail route. At the village school car park walk into the main street, the WC is signed, approximately 30 metres up-hill from the shop/Post Office.

Birdoswald Roman Fort. On the Trail. Permissive WC (& water tap) located in the site's courtyard, ask at reception desk. Available normal opening hours. (Also café, and passport stamping station, see the relevant lists).

Sands Sports Centre. Telephone 01228 625222. On the Trail. WC in reception area. Open: 09.00 to 21.30 daily.

Drumburgh, the Grange farm. Telephone 01228 576551. Permissive WC, also drinks vending machine, and permissive water tap (see relevant lists). On the Trail, located up cul-de-sac opposite junction in village, from where it will be signed. Open: 08.00 to 17.00, other times by arrangement.

Port Carlisle, Solway Methodist Church. A quiet place for retreat. Permissive water tap and WC available. Open: May - Aug from morning to early evening.

Bowness-on-Solway. WC available in the village hall. Next to the King's Arms. Open daily in daylight hours from approx 09.30.

Shops and Post Offices

When you sit down to plan your trip do make a note of where all the shops are. You will, of course, find plenty of food shops in Wallsend, Newcastle and Carlisle and it is not practicable to mention them all, so this list is selective. We have tried to include every general store, post office and anything else that we think you need to know about either on the Trail itself, or within easy reach of it. Some walkers' tips from 2003 are recommended. Where the larger settlements have a wider range of shops this is indicated. Many of the shops are also Post Offices. They are particularly useful if you bank with Alliance and Leicester, Barclays, Cahoot, Co-op, Lloyds TSB or Smile because you can also **draw out cash from them**. You will need your ATM card and your pin number. The Post Office hours are not necessarily the same as the shop opening hours so please take note. Note that every Post Office now sells **electronic mobile phone top-ups.** (See also the separate section on obtaining money).

Tyneside and Northumberland

Wallsend

Nearest Metro station is Wallsend. Contains a wide range of general shops and supermarkets. Because you might be stocking up on provisions here the two supermarkets nearest to Segedunum are mentioned.

Kwik Save. One minute's walk from Segedunum, standing outside the main gate look across the road to your right. Open: Mon - Wed 08.00 to 19.00; Thurs - Fri 08.00 to 20.00; Sat 08.00 to 18.00; Sun 10.00 to 16.00. **Cashback & mobile phone top-ups.**

Co-op. The Forum shopping centre. Five minutes walk from Segedunum, from the site walk up Station Road to the traffic lights, the Forum is across the road to your left. Open: Mon - Sat 08.00 to 20.00. Sun 10.00 to 16.00. **Cashback & mobile phone top-ups.**

Post Office. Located inside the Co-op. Telephone: 0191 263 0642. Open: Mon-Fri 0800 to 1730. Sat 09.00 to 15.00.

Newcastle city centre

Contains the range of shops, supermarkets, restaurants etc. that you would expect to find in a city centre. The nearest supermarket to the Trail is **Safeway in Nelson Street** (nearest Metro station is Monument). Opposite Safeway is the famous Grainger Market where you will find the most competitively priced fruit and vegetables (amongst other things) in the north of England. To get to Nelson Street, from the Tyne bridge walk up Dean Street into Grey Street, turning left into Market Street. This brings you to Grainger Street, turn right then first left into Nelson Street. There is also a **Post Office** to be found inside the entrance to Eldon Square shopping centre. Open: Mon - Sat 09.00 to 17.30.

Newcastle Business Park

Riverside Newsagent. Telephone 0191 226 0686. Open: Mon - Fri 07.00 to 16.30. Sat 08.00 to 12.00. Located only 30 metres from the route, across the adjacent road, a short distance west of Dunstan Staithes (large pier structure in the River Tyne). You will also find a café bar and deli. (See page 53).

Newburn

(No general shops apart from a fish and chip shop and newsagent).

Post Office, Station Road. Open: Mon & Tue 08.30 to 17.30. Wed 08.00 to 17.00. Thurs & Fri 08.30 to 17.30. Sat 08.30 to 12.30.

Heddon-on-the-Wall

General store. Telephone: 01661 853976. Open Mon - Fri: 08.00 to 18.00; Sat 08.00 to 17.00; Sun 09.00 to 12.00.

Post Office and newsagent, also off-licence. Telephone: 01661 853433.
Shop open: Mon - Sat: 07.15 to 18.00; Sun: 07.15 to 12.00.
Post office open: Mon - Fri 09.00 to 17.30; Sat 09.00 to 12.30.

Dingle Dell Delicatessen (and Tea Room). Telephone: 01661 854 325. Open: Mon - Fri 09.00 to 17.30; Sat 09.30 to 16.30; and Sunday afternoons.

Spar Supermarket and Shell garage. Telephone 01661 852276. Open: Mon - Sat 07.00 to 21.00; Sun 08.00 to 20.00. Also cash machine inside shop (UK banks only) for which a charge is made; permissive WC & water tap (see relevant lists). **Mobile phone electronic top-ups.**

Wylam

Spar supermarket. Telephone 01661 852214. Open Sun - Sat: 06.00 to 21.00. **Cashback facility & mobile phone top-ups.**

Post Office. Telephone 01661 852241. Open Mon - Tues: 09.00 to 12.00pm & 13.30 to 17.30. Wed 09.00 to 12.00. Thurs - Fri: 09.00 to 12.00 & 13.30 to 17.30. Sat: 09.00 to 12.00.

Delicatessen and Tea Shop. Telephone 01661 852552. Shop open Mon - Sat: 07.30 to 17.30. Sun: 10.30 to 17.00. Tea room open: Mon - Sat: 08.00 to 16.15. Sun: 10.30 to 16.15.

Corbridge

Contains a small range of general shops.

Walter Wilson supermarket (now a Co-op), Hill Street. Telephone 01434 632007. Open: Mon - Sat 07.00 to 22.00. Sun 08.00 to 22.00. **Cashback facility.**

Post Office and newsagent. Town Hall Buildings. Newsagent open: Mon - Fri 05.00 to 17.30. Sat 05.00 to 18.00. Sun 05.00 to 12.30. Post Office open: Mon - Fri 08.30 to 17.30. Sat 08.30 to 12.30. Telephone: 01434 632042.

Acomb

Post Office and Shop. Telephone 01434 603743. Open: Mon, Tues, Thurs, Fri: 09.00 to 17.30 (closed for lunch 12.30 to 13.30). Wed: 09.00 to 13.00. Sat: 09.00 to 12.30.

The Village Shop. South west edge of village, on the A6079 road. Telephone 01434 603810. Open: daily 06.00 to 12.30.

Hexham

Contains a wide range of supermarkets and general shops, restaurants etc.

Post Office. Fore Street. (Within Robb's department store which also includes a supermarket). Telephone 01434 602001. Post Office open: Mon - Tues 08.30 to 17.30; Wed 09.00 to 17.30; Thurs 08.30 to 17.30; Fri 08.30 to 18.00; Sat 08.30 to 17.00.

Humshaugh

Post Office and general store. Telephone 01434 681258. Post office open: Mon 09.00 to 12.00 & 13.00 to 17.00. Tues to Fri 09.00 to 13.00. Sat 09.00 to 12.00.

Shop open: Mon 07.30 to 17.00. Tues to Fri 07.30 to 13.00. Sat 07.30 to 12.00. Sun 09.00 to 12.00.

Haydon Bridge

Co-op and Post Office. Telephone 01434 684327. Shop & Post Office open: Sun 09.00 to 22.00; Mon & Tues 08.00 to 22.00; Wed 08.00 to 22.00 (post office to 21.00); Thurs - Sat 08.00 to 22.00. **Electronic mobile phone top-ups**.

Turret 34a

Sewing Shields Farm. Grid ref: NY 809 703. A drinks vending machine will open in 2004. Look out for sign by the farm.

Haltwhistle

Contains a wide range of general shops

Post Office. Main Street. Telephone 01434 320361. Open: Mon - Fri 09.00 to 17.30. Sat 09.00 to 12.00.

Co-op supermarket. Main Street. Telephone 01434 321188. Open: Mon - Sat 08.00 to 22.00. Sun 10.00 to 16.00. **Cashback facility**.

Quality Fayre supermarket. Telephone 01434 320392. Open: Mon - Sat: 08.00 to 21.45. Sun: 10.00 to 16.00. **Cashback facility.**

Cumbria

Gilsland

Post Office and general store. Telephone 016977 47011. Post office open: Mon - Wed 09.00 to 12.30 & 13.30 to 17.30. Thurs 09.00 to 12.30. Fri 09.00 to 12.30 & 13.30 to 17.30. Sat 09.00 to 12.30.

Shop open: Mon - Wed 07.30 to 12.30 & 13.30 to 17.30. Thurs 07.30 to 12.30. Fri 07.30 to 12.30 & 13.30 to 17.30. Sat 07.30 to 12.30.

Brampton

Brampton Post Office (in Mitchellson's Newsagents). Telephone 016977 2301. Open: Mon - Fri 09.00 to 17.30. Sat 09.00 to 12.30.

Irthington

Post Office and shop. Telephone 016977 2300. Post office is normally open the same times as for the shop: Mon - Fri 08.45 to 12.30 & 13.00 to 18.30; Sat 08.45 to 13.00; Sun 09.30 to 12.30.

Carlisle

Expect to find an extensive range of shops in this bustling city centre.

Main Post Office. Warwick Road (Near Railway Station). Open: Mon - Sat 09.00 to 17.30.

Post Office and Shop, Scotch Street. Telephone 01228 525017. Open: Mon - Fri 09.00 to 17.30. Sat 09.00 to 17.00.

Burgh-by-Sands

Post Office and shop. Telephone 01228 576342. Open: Mon & Thurs 09.00 to 12.00 & 15.00 to 17.00.

Drumburgh

The Grange farm. Telephone 01228 576551. Drinks vending machine, also permissive water tap and WC. Located up cul-de-sac opposite junction in village, from where it will be signed. Open: 08.00 to 17.00, other times by arrangement.

0.5 (0.8 km) mile east of Port Carlisle

Glendale Caravan Park. Telephone 016973 51317. Site general shop open to walkers; non-accredited camping (see page 37). Grid ref: NY 244 612.

Bowness-on-Solway

Post Office. Open: Mon & Thur 09.30 to 12.30 and 14.00 to 16.00.

Cafés (and other places where you will find refreshments)

This list excludes pubs and restaurants. There are several cafés on or close to the Trail as well as other places that offer some form of refreshment that we have decided to include in this list. Note their opening times and arrangements.

Tyneside and Northumberland

Wallsend

Cafés and places to eat are numerous in High Street and in the Forum shopping centre. As a general rule the cafés are shut all day Sunday.

Segedunum Roman Fort. Café available during opening hours. See list of historic sites, museums and visitor centres for full details of site.

Newcastle Quayside.

Ouseburn Watersports Association. Telephone 0191 224 3832. (There are several places to eat along the Quayside, but this place has been recommended by walkers). This boating club welcomes walkers for hot and cold drinks and food. It is located five minutes walk west of the huge Spillers Flour Mill on the Quayside. Look out for the flotilla of small boats moored by the quay. Open: 10.00 to 23.00 Weds - Mon. Closed Tues.

Wylam Waggonway

Stephenson's birthplace cottage. Telephone 01661 853457. This National Trust site, situated on the Wylam Waggonway, is approx 0.5 mile (0.8 km) west of the Trail at GR NZ 126 650, and less than a mile (approx 1 km) from Wylam (shop; café; pharmacy; pubs) where many walkers find accommodation. It is the birthplace of George Stephenson and so, quite literally therefore, the cradle of the railway age. Besides the interest in the site itself (it is also haunted) a delightful small tea room, whose staff sometimes dress in period costume, will assure you of a warm welcome. The cottage is open from 1st April to 1st Nov, Thurs - Sun, 13.00 to 17.00. The tea room is open 12.00 to 17.00. If your itinerary allows you the time, the combination of the café and historic interest makes this a top tip.

Newcastle Business Park

You will find the following premises approx 30 metres across the adjacent road from the Trail, a short way to the west of Dunston Staithes (a large pier structure in the river Tyne).

Bar Escape. Telephone 0191 272 0345. Open Mon - Fri 09.30 to 19.30; Sat - Sun 11.00 to 17.00.

The Deli. Telephone 0191 272 0544. Open: Mon - Fri 07.00 to 15.00.

Heddon-on-the-Wall

Dingle Dell Tea Room. (Look out for a sign in the village to Heddon shopping centre). Telephone 01661 854325. Open: Mon - Fri 09.00 to 17.30. Sat 09.30 to 16.30 Please telephone to check for Sunday hours.

Wylam

Tea Shop & Delicatessen. Telephone 01661 852552. Tea shop open: Mon - Sat 08.00 to 16.15. Sun 10.30 to 16.15.

Chip Van: every Wednesday from 5pm to 7pm, across the road from the Spar supermarket.

Wylam Diner, 41-43 Jackson Street. 01661 852672. Chinese takeaway.

Corbridge

The Art Café, Market place. Telephone 01434 634090. Open: 10.00 to 17.00 daily.

Chadwick's Tea Rooms. Middle Street. Telephone 01434 632429. Open: Tues - Sat 09.00 to 17.00. Closed Sun & Mon.

Watling Coffee Shop. Watling Street. Telephone 01434 633095. Open: Mon - Fri 10.00 to 17.00. Sat 10.00 to 17.30. Closed Sun.

Gresham Garden tea rooms, Market Square. Open: Fri - Sun 10.00 to 17.00. Also open main school holidays (normally last week of July, all of August and first week of September).

Corbridge Sandwich Bar, Middle Street. Telephone 01434 634000. Open: daily 08.30 to 16.00.

B6318 Military Road

St. Oswald's Café. Telephone 01434 689010. On the Trail. Grid ref: NY 940 694. Open: March/April/Nov Fri, Sat, Sun 10.00 to 16.30. May - Oct, daily 10.00 to 16.30. Closed Mon.

Chollerford

Riverside Tea Rooms. Telephone 01434 681325. Next to garage, on west side of roundabout. Open: Daily 08.30 - 16.00. Internet access.

Luculus Larder, Chesters Roman Fort. Telephone 01434 681781. Open: April - October 10.00 to 17.00. (N.B. For use of Chesters Fort visitors only).

B6318 Military Road, Northumberland National Park

Housesteads Roman Fort. (Joint National Trust/English Heritage). National Trust shop, info centre and refreshments kiosk. Telephone 01434 344525. Open: daily April - Oct 10.00 to 18.00; rest of year 10.00 to 16.00.

(Closed Christmas/Boxing Day and New Year's Day).

Once Brewed

Once Brewed Visitor Centre. Telephone 01434 344396. Open: April - Oct 09.00 to 17.00 daily. Open weekends in winter. Internet access. Hot drinks vending machine only.

Greenhead

Ye Olde Forge Tea Rooms. Telephone 016977 47174. Open: March - April, Oct - Dec 10.00 to 16.00. May - Sept 09.00 to 17.00.

Haltwhistle

Truly Scrumptious Sandwich Bar. Telephone 01434 321321. Main Street. Open: Mon - Sat 08.00 to 14.30.

Gilsland

Dacre House Tea Room. Telephone 016977 47371. Walk into Gilsland village main street from either the village school car park or the Station Hotel car park. Open: Wed - Sun 10.00 to 16.00. Closed Mon and Tues.

Birdoswald Roman Fort. Telephone 016977 47602. Open: 1 March - 9 November 10.00 to 17.30 daily (last admission 17.00). Tea Room open: 10.00 to 17.00. Internet access. (Also permissive WC and water tap, passport stamping station. www.birdoswaldromanfort.org

Lanercost

Haytongate. Telephone 016977 41119 (weekday office hours). Grid ref: NY 554 645. Hot and cold drinks available when notice is displayed.

Brampton

Routledges Bakers. Telephone 016977 41555. Open: Mon - Thurs 08.30 to 16.30. Fri 08.00 to 16.30. Sat 08.00 to 15.00.

Capon Tree Café, Front Street. Telephone 016977 3649. Open: Mon - Sat 09.15 to 16.30.

The Bread Shop. Telephone 016977 2919. Open: Mon - Fri 08.00 to 16.30. Sat 08.00 to 16.00.

Carlisle

Café at the Sands Sports Centre. Telephone 01228 625526. Open: 10.00 to 21.00 daily (Sports Centre open 09.00 to 21.30). Also permissive water tap (see page 44). On the Trail, also a passport stamping station.

Port Carlisle

Marshmallow Tea Room. Custom House. Telephone 016973 52300. Open: Tues - Sun 11.00 to 17.00. Closed Mon.

This list includes the pubs with restaurants actually on the route itself or close enough to be useful to you. Rest assured that there are many more in the surrounding towns and villages where you are likely to spend your evenings.

Tyneside and Northumberland

Newburn

The Keelmans. Telephone 0191 267 0772. Open: Mon - Sat 11.00 - 23.00; Sun 12.00 to 22.30. Food served: 12.00 to 21.00 daily. Location: Grange Road; from the boat launch slipway walk towards the Visitor Centre, turn right, the pub is two minutes walk on the left.

Heddon-on-the-Wall

Three Tuns. Telephone 01661 852172. Open: 10.00 to 23.00 daily. Food served: 12.00 to 14.30 daily.

The Swan. Telephone 01661 853161. Open: Mon - Sat 11.00 to 23.00, Sun 12.00 to 22.30. Food served: Mon - Sat 12.00 to 21.15, Sun 12.00 to 19.30.

B6318 Military Road

Robin Hood Inn. Approx one mile (1.6 km) west of the Whittledene reservoirs on the B6318. Grid ref: NZ 050 684. Open: Mon - Thurs 12.00 to 15.00 & 18.00 to 23.00; Fri, Sat 12.00 to 23.00; Sun 12.00 to 22.30. Food served: Mon - Fri 12.00 to 14.30 & 18.00 to 21.30; Sat 12.00 - 21.30; Sun 12.00 to 16.00 (Sunday lunch) & 17.00 to 21.00.

Errington Arms. Telephone 01434 672250. West side of the A68 roundabout. Grid ref: NY 987 686. Open: 11.00 to 15.00 & 18.00 to 23.00 (Closed Sunday evening and Monday all day). Food served: 12.00 to 14.30 & 18.30 to 21.30, Sunday lunch 12.00 to 15.00.

Corbridge

Has several pubs and restaurants that serve food.

Wall village

The Hadrian. Telephone 01434 681232. Grid ref: NY 916 688. Open: 11.00 to 23.00 daily. Food served: 12.00 to 20.45 daily.

Chollerford

The George Hotel. Telephone 01434 681611. Bar Open: 11.00 to 23.00 daily. Food served: 18.30 to 21.00 daily. Snacks served: 07.00 to 17.00 daily. Breakfast Available: Mon - Fri 07.00 to 09.00, Sat 07.00 to 10.00, Sun 08.00 to 10.00.

Humshaugh

The Crown Inn. Telephone 01434 681231. Open: Mon - Tues 18.00 to 23.00. Wed - Fri 12.00 to 14.30 & 18.00 to 23.00. Sat 12.00 to 23.00. Sun 12.00 to 22.30. Food Served: Wed - Fri 12.00 to 14.30 & 18.00 to 21.00. Sat 12.00 to 14.00 &18.00 to 21.00. Sunday lunch 12.00 to 15.00. No smoking area available upon request.

Hexham

There are several pubs, takeaways and restaurants in Hexham including a JD Wetherspoon pub, The Forum in Market Place, where (walker's tip) you can eat in a smoke free environment.

Once Brewed

Twice Brewed Inn. Telephone 01434 344534. Grid ref: NY 752 669. Open: Mon - Sat 11.00 to 23.00. Sun 12.00 to 22.30. Food served: All day until 20.30. Walkers breakfast available: Easter - End Sept 8.00 to 9.00. No smoking restaurant. Disabled toilet. Internet facility.

B6318 Military Road

Milecastle Inn. Telephone 01434 321372. 0.5 mile (0.8 km) from Cawfields car park Milecastle 42. Grid ref: NY 716 660. Open: 11.00 to 23.00 daily, April to October. Food served 11.00 to 21.00 daily.

Haltwhistle

Has several pubs and restaurants that serve food.

Greenhead

Greenhead Hotel. Telephone 016977 47411. Grid ref: NY 660 654. Open: 12.00 to 23.00 daily. Food served: 12.00 to 20.30 daily. Sunday lunch served all day Sunday. No smoking area available.

Cumbria

Gilsland

Station Hotel. Telephone 016977 47338. Open: 12.00 to 23.00 daily. Food served: 12.00 to 21.00 daily. Walkers may use facilities and fill their water bottles here.

Samson Inn. Telephone 016977 47220. Open: 12.00 to 23.00 daily. Food served: 12.00 to 21.00 daily.

Bridge Inn. Telephone 016977 47353. Open: 12.00 to 23.00 daily. Food served: 12.00 to 14.00 & 18.00 to 20.00 daily.

Lanercost

Abbey Bridge Inn. Telephone 016977 2224. (This pub and restaurant is very handy if you have finished a section at Haytongate (GR NY 553 645). It is about a mile (1.6 km) from the Trail and close to Lanercost Priory where the AD 122 bus stops. Open daily: 12.00 to 15.00 & 18.00 to 23.00. Food served: 12.00 to 14.00 & 18.30 to 21.00.

Walton

The Centurion. Telephone 016977 2438. Open: 10.00 to 23.00 daily. Bar meals served: 12.00 to 21.00 daily. Lunch menu served: 12.00 to 14.30 daily. All day Sunday lunch from 12.00 to 21.00. On the Trail.

Laversdale

The Sportsman. Telephone 01228 573255. Open: 12.00 to 23.00 daily. Food 12.00 to 21.00. Pick-up service from Old Wall by arrangement. Internet facility. Also, non-accredited camping at rear. Pub located approx one mile (1.6 km) from GR 488 618 - link signed as a bridle way.

Irthington

Approx 0.6 mile (1 km) from GR 488 618 - signed as a bridleway. There is also a shop/Post Office (see page 51).

Salutation Inn. Telephone 016977 2310. Open: Mon evening 17.00 to 23.00 (Closed Monday lunch); Tues - Fri 12.00 to 15.00 & 17.00 to 23.00. Sat & Sun 12.00 to 23.00. Please check for the availability of food.

Crosby

Stag Inn. Telephone 01228 573210. Open: 11.00 to 23.00 daily. Food served: 12.00 to 14.00 & 18.00 to 21.00 daily. Refreshments for walkers available from 10.00 every morning.

Carlisle

You will find a large selection of pubs and restaurants in Carlisle.

Burgh by Sands

The Greyhound. Telephone 01228 576579. Open: Mon - Fri 12.00 to 14.00 & 17.00 to 23.00. Sat, Sun 11.00 to 23.00. Snacks at all times, hot meals: Fri, Sat 12.00 to 14.00 & 17.00 to 20.00.

Glasson

Highland Laddie. Telephone 016973 51839. Open: 12.00 to 16.00 & 18.00 to 23.00 daily, but closed Tuesday lunchtime. Food served lunchtimes and evenings, telephone to check availability.

Port Carlisle

Hope and Anchor. Telephone 016973 51460. Open 11.00 to 23.00 daily. Food served: 12.00 to 15.00 & 18.00 to 21.00 daily. No smoking area in restaurant.

Bowness-on-Solway

The King's Arms. Telephone 016973 51426. Also passport stamping station. Open daily 11.00 to 23.00. Hot meals 12.00 to 14.00. Sandwiches after 14.00. Bar meals 18.00 to 21.00.

Hadrian's Wall Path Trust

A new membership-based organisation, the Hadrian's Wall Path Trust, was launched in the spring of 2004. The Trust's aims, in recognition of the pre-eminence, uniqueness and vulnerability of Hadrian's Wall World Heritage Site, are threefold:

1. To promote the recreational and educational value of the National Trail in a way that is archaeologically, environmentally and economically sustainable.

2. To provide a forum for visitors and locals alike, indeed anyone with an interest in the Trail, to contribute ideas and enthusiasm towards the long-term well being of both the World Heritage Site and its Path.

3. To make representation to: national or local government, businesses, organisations or individuals in order to achieve these aims.

For the latest news on the Trust's launch and details of membership please check the National Trail website at:

www.nationaltrail.co.uk/hadrianswall

Notes